DRY SWALLOW

Camilla Marquette

Dry Swallow

Flammarion Prints
ISBN: 1732464901
ISBN-13: 978-1732464902

Cover art by Georgia Tell

Original cover image was created by the Internet Archive Book Images as digitization of an image on page 123 of John Charles Buckmaster's 1873 book *Elements of Animal Physiology, Chiefly Human*. The author asserts no affiliation with Internet Archive Book Images or any other entities involved in the making of this image.

This image is available on Flickr at: https://www.flickr.com/photos/internetarchivebookimages/14596119050/. Images used in cover art are in the public domain.

To contact the author, send an email to flammarion.prints@gmail.com.

For the space cadets.

— *C. M.*

DRY SWALLOW

DRY SWALLOW

dry swallow
◀◀ ● ▶▶

I
Like Lungs, We

Invocation of the Muse

Consider the journal
you started two years ago,
the majority of its pages still blank,

and tell me again
that you have anything noteworthy
to say.

Domain and Range

a·poc·a·lypse, from /ἀποκάλυψις/ (pl. **apocalypses**)
1 a sudden divulgence of knowledge, or the revelation of
something hidden **2** a cycle of destruction followed by
rebirth, on repeat, ad infinitum **3** the snake, eating dust,
swallowing its own tail

II
Collapse,

Critical Mass

There is no air in Quartzsite, Arizona,
It's liquid heat and dust that fills airbag lungs.
Copper weather tastes like sucking a paper cut.
Out here, avoid eye contact with the stones.

The only things in motion are the highway,
And faded candy wrappers caught in a hot gust,
And you. The patient vulture on the post
Watches with one obsidian eye.

Nobody gets all the way through the desert
Without pausing here for fuel. Pump quickly,
Suck shallow lungfuls and just try to ignore
The accusatory finger of the snowless mountaintops.

Semis barrel down the road, a constant
Violent machete hacking. This red place
Split at the seams like a ruptured lung.
You didn't do it, but nonetheless, the rust sets in.

Amid the dull automotive roar you hear
The vulture, perched on a tombstone, laughing
Hollowly, singing "Not with a bang, never a bang.
How's life in the whimper, kid?" Parched throat.
He winks.

The Birth of God

Was thirsty, so I drank the ocean
Hungry, so I ate the moon
Mad, so quaked a big commotion
Chilly, so I made it June

Sleepy, so I dozed on Saturn
Dirty, so I bathed in dew
Lost, so made the Sun my lantern
Lonely, so I thought up You

Made Your belly out of daydreams
Used hailstorms for Your eyes
Fed You quasars 'til You ran in streams
Down endless mountainsides

Named the space between us "cosmos"
Called Your sweet breath "revolution"
Painted righteous fear on one palm
On the other, Love's solution

Bade You stand, and so You stood up
Called Your name, and so You came
In place of wine brought You a cup
Of my self, which You drained

Thought You'd hold me, but You hit me
Thought You'd mend – instead, You broke
Made a sword out of my long teeth
Watched me bleed out at Your blow

Now I don't thirst, so I don't drink
Am not hungry, dirty, or lost
Simply float alone at daybreak
And shudder at the cost

What Happened, v. 1

In the summertime, he was okay,
Stood on his own, occasionally
Paused beneath to escape the heat of the day in her shade.

"Use me," the willow encouraged him
Because she loved him.

As the days turned cold, the preacher began
To worry about how he would survive the winter's freeze

      And what was she doing anyways,
      Besides just standing there,
      Digging her heels into the dirt?

At the first snowfall, the preacher chopped
Off one limb, split it into tiny pieces
Made himself a fire that lasted all week.

Then he did it again, and the willow
Wept heavy sap from the stubs, but still
She wanted him to be warm.

After that, the preacher
Not yet content with the heat her body provided him,
Grabbed his ax and climbed to the top of her,

Plucked willowy branches from her
One by one by one by one by one
Wove them into a roof.

She creaked her protests but the preacher, oblivious,
Brought the ax down again and again
And again and again and again
Until he had felled every limb and split
Her bosom in two.

And then to her trunk and
With one last wail,
The willow toppled.

It wasn't the preacher's fault
The warm hollow of her had been given freely,
Because, as she had said, once, she loved him.

     And besides, what had she been doing anyways
     Except just standing there and
     Reaching for the stars?

road trip through the wastelands

Order the soft pretzel and lick off all the salt

Dunk the bread in nacho cheese mixed with ketchup and suck off the sauce

Then throw the tray and the paper cup and the bread in the trash like no one anywhere is starving

Like everything's starfish - cut it in half and regenerate a forest on the spot

Single-use coffee cups and Redbull cans

Forming avalanches in the passenger side of the car your parents gave you at graduation,

Like a trickle-down addiction - neon urine and caffeine headaches

Like we aren't almost out of air

Gills gasping for oxygen in a dark bubbling puddle

Push the pedal all the way down and go faster,

Burn through the remnants of ancient redwoods and the remains of lumbering brontosaurs,

Like it's no big deal dashing through all of Arizona in one day

Like those are just storm clouds and

No harm in taking a lungful

Chew hangnails in dry chunks off your thumb and

Scrape dead skin off your bottom lip with your teeth

Like you are sloughing barnacles off a ship hull,

Like you aren't made up of a million separate bits,

Fuel just waiting to be digested

Failure to Thrive

The dead kitten in the back seat is no one's fault,
It's just that glass, fallen from a height, has a tendency
to shatter.

Hourglass

At first there is a butterfly, then, a chrysalis, then
a slug drops out of the air like a silver stone.
Turns out that when the winds can
no longer carry you, they cut
you. Erosion like finally
swallowing the lump
in your throat, like
gulping sharp
stones, like
sand
weighing all
the fluttery parts
down. Sure, you may
remember what it felt like
to fly, but zoom in too close and
turns out the big picture is just pixels.
Turns out the only difference between the slug
and the granules that grind the heavy body to sand
is a lifetime of being worn down and converted, dust to dust.

Id

The librarian hates books
Absolutely loathes them.
Wants to spend all her time
Wrapping their knowledge into neat packages,
Listing their names in quiet, clean catalogs,
Stacking them in order on the shelves
Where they can do no further harm,
Shushing them so they cause no further noise.

What Happened, v.2

Step-mother doesn't know why
Little bird has started pulling out all her feathers.
Step-mother doesn't understand why
Little bird can't keep swallowing away
Her bright happiness like a placebo.

Spare Change

The three pigeons look quizzically, cock their heads.
One bares teeth like a million stripped wires
arranged haphazardly in an underbite.

I reach into my pocket and pelt them
with a hundred heavy nickels and silver dollars, whereby,
straining, neck veins bulging under matted grey feathers
they lift into the sky with calloused claws and dry beating
wings.

Vigilante

The first sundial was a mistake; the first clock, a violence.
Timekeepers infiltrating our comfortable daze like wild ivy
Scaling the walls, wrapping around our wrists and filling our
pockets
Pervasive like the itch you keep on scratching,
Like the pill you can't stop swallowing.

If I had the chance, I'd kick over that first sundial,
Slap the first clock out of the first clockmaker's palm and
watch the gears scatter on the stone floor.
Stop the fools from spinning up the galaxy,
From setting the solar system in its vast motion,
From starting the world turning in its incessant manner,
From waking up Time
And making us mortal.

Negative Reinforcement

"This will prove
that I love them,"
God mused,
stoking the coals.

Ego

The librarian would very much like
For the earth to be flat, thank you.

She knows it isn't, of course.
But how convenient it would be
To be able to fold the entire planet
Hamburger-style, once, twice,
Slip it in to her front shirt pocket and
Go about the day holding everything
Worth believing on a single sheet.

Globes, unfortunately, are not so easy
To condense to a single dimension.
Much to her chagrin, it is impossible
To reduce reality to one basic truth.

Attack

Called it an "attack"
As if the panic ever
Truly loses hold.

What Happened, v.3

It wasn't that it was rotten the whole way through,
But the pace
– God, the pace of things was suffocating.

It stuck to her feathers and matted them together,
Weighted her wings so she flew like a bloated buzzard,
Coated the back of her throat like thick medicine
She could barely breathe around the lump there.

Night after night, the preacher sat and
Flicked his silver tongue over the temple braille,
Swallowed stone after stone until his eyes turned dark, and misty
Drank bowl after bowl of sweet honey until it filled him to the brim
Overflowed out his nostrils.

Stop!, she would shout at him
stop, stop, stop
– For she could see he was drowning.

(Some nights, when the honey flowed out of his dark eyes
He would swallow her, too.

It took her one thousand years, but she finally climbed out
of the preacher's maw.)

Left him to his rocks and liquors and strange ruins
Spent the next centuries coughing thick liquid out of her lungs,
Stretching her loosened wings.

With this freedom so hard-won, she couldn't understand
Why her wings still so often felt heavy, and dull,
Why she still had to swallow around the lump in her throat,
Craving the suffocation of something sickly-sweet.

Spare Us the Eulogy

All this chaos,
a hive of minds shouting grey TV static.

Why do you move to speak?

How dare you
add your voice
to the senseless white noise?

Shut your mouth,
close your throat and your eyes and
lie down in your hole.

Pull the dirt comforter over your head
to stifle the poetry,

press your soiled hands together in silent prayer
and just wait
until the feeling passes.

Looking down from a high place

What kind of a sin is
the temptation of
standing at the edge
of the hiking path
the urge to take one
more step off?

> *What if I turn the wheel*
> *just so, just now?*

> *What if I unclip the tether,*
> *float away into cold space*
> *or down into deep ocean?*

What do you call the wretch
who forgets their neighbor's gold
and covets the neighbor's graveplot instead?

Tombstone vs. Eulogy

Trees write their stories on stones, not papers
because they know their own propensity for decay

*

the stars are not ashamed of me
worse
they are indifferent

III
Expand,

On cycles

Spinning new universes in the back seat of the Honda Civic
Dollar store kaleidoscope against one eye and seat belt
buckle against my ribs.

Though at first the shifting patterns seem unique
It doesn't take long for the shapes to begin repeating,

Like the unbroken lines of trees rushing by endlessly out
the window,
Or the way I keep turning my thoughts inside and outside,
Living in a cosmos the size of an anxiety attack
And then in a cosmos the size of infinity and full of
impossible color.

Zoom in, zoom out
Zoom in, zoom out

Each new point of view seems rare until the fractal
coalesces.
Each new song sounds distinct until the Aeolian harp
exhausts its range.

On outliers

Of all the girls,
with all the bifocals,
and all the half-eaten pretzels,
in all the parking lots,
in all the greater LA metro area,

you.

What Happened, v.4

Folk wisdom says that time heals all wounds
But it still hasn't been a full year since last June
So I fear that this gash in the side of my heart is still gaping.

The pain ebbs and flows, and may go away soon
But it's still only been seven months since last June
So right now the whole at the center of me is still breaking.

I'm miles away here from the ground zero ruins
But still not far enough from what you said last June
So you see why I just keep on walking without hesitating.

The one hope I've held that I know to be true
Is that one day I'll turn and look back at last June
And all the sharp edges, and you, will be paler, and fading.

driving the Sierras

If the mountain is a molar,
The highway isn't a cavity.
It can't be.

It has to be something more hopeful,
Like a vein of gold in granite,
Or the white foam of a cresting wave.

And if it is a cavity,
It has to be something we can root out,
Restoring the mantle to full strength.
The crack cannot go to the core
It just can't.

Sermon on the Mount

If summer days are rays of sunlight endless,
Then winter's dusk is built from tombstone bricks.
If chains are gonna bind you up regardless,
Then who are you to stand up and resist?

Nobody gets to choose the mold they're smelt in
These times of fire singe the strides we've made.
The seasons change, and we've no power to pause them.
The trees all burn except what seeds we save.

Tonight, I stand here at the cusp of autumn,
The night is red with flames, the moon is full
Of questions, hopes and dreams I've long forgotten.
The stars are heartmeat cast off from the whole.

And yet – the violent cycle still surprises,
For though the fire destroys, the smoke rises.

A Lovesong for the Post-Apocalypse

Oh my love, you are the light of my life,
Which is especially helpful because
The thermonuclear winter blocking the sun makes it pretty hard
to see.

Your hair, beautiful one, is a thick, luxurious tangle,
Not unlike the carnivorous, genetically-modified super-vine
Currently scaling the crumbled remains of the Empire State
building.

Your dark eyes, dear one, are as black and as deep
As the gaping yaw of the endless void from which
We hapless creatures sprung and into which we all invariably
return.

And your lips – oh, my love, your lips –
Are as red as the fresh blood dribbling
Down a zombie's chin to his chest after a recent and gory
feasting.

Your body is curved and comfortable, my sweet.
It keeps me warm at night,
Probably because after the nukes we're all radioactive now.
Darling, your skin literally glows!

When I hold you in my arms, my peach, I feel you tenderly
trembling
And not just in fear as the robot overlords crash through our
encampment with their scalping knives.

When I see you delicately gunning down an old lady for a can of food, precious one,

You take my breath away even more than the polluted, CO^2-soaked atmosphere normally does.

When I kiss you, sweet angel, it is like taking a long, cool drink from a clean spring

Which I especially enjoy since most of the water I drink these days is acid rainwater and ash.

And now, standing with you here at the edge of the end of the world,

Staring head-on into the eternal abyss

— whose inevitable embrace often seems a thing to desire more than fear, since it will at least mean a release from the agony of this weaponized bioengineered plague we've contracted —

Standing here, in this tortured, desert hellscape,

That we neither created nor asked to be a part of,

I can't help but think that this life has nonetheless been worth it,

Because you are here to share this God-forsaken place with me.

My love, you are all the starlight that somehow manages to filter in

Through the thick of the angry, heat-soaked clouds —

Meaningless in the scheme of things but all the reason there has ever been

To look up.

Lightheaded

the world hasn't ended

(at least, I've not heard anything on the news)
but it sure is strange?
about the clocks?
all stopped, all broken the whole world over
probably right twice a day
but without knowing the time, nobody can be sure.

and the radio static filling the air, crackling endlessly
is certainly odd, and annoying
as is the way the lines of the chair keep blending
into the lines of the floor and the lines of the wall
which makes it impossible to sit for a breather,
you know?

this isn't the end of the world for sure but it's definitely
the start of something

Archives

Beneath rich soil
Tree roots transfer their stories
From stump to sapling

The Determinist

Common knowledge among cartographers is that
All maps lie. If every minute detail of the land was drawn
into a map of Japan,
You'd need a tabletop the size of Japan just to unfurl it on.

It is stupid to call the crystal "magic"
When "isometric-hexoctahedral carbon-14" is its proper
name.
Eventually, minds and diamonds decompose into the same
basic stuff.

Birds in the sky, fish in the sea.
Roots in the dirt, branches in the air.
The nature of the niche predicts with infallible accuracy
how it will be exploited.

Eternity is reducible
To yes-no, on-off, in-out, up-down.
The truth is told in 1s and 0s, if it can be told at all.

Heat defines cold, sound invents silence,
In a blaze, light shears from itself something that can now
be called darkness.
The most dazzling singularity will expose its torpid binary if
you zoom in close enough.

There is a danger in believing
That the spider weaves a web when all she does is
Tie the same knot over and over and over again.

Concuss the cosmos inside out and you will find
That from the very first bang, it is determined
Which molecules of saltwater will form the oceans and
which will form your tears.

What Happened, v. 5

Even once she is freed, little bird does not sing, does not eat
But flies to the highest peak of the preacher's house,
Makes a nest there out of some bark and her few remaining feathers,
And sits there, day and night, day and night
Season after season after season
Trying to convince herself, whispering
"We did the best we could"
"We did what we had to do"
While the dilapidated house moans its solemn concurrence
With each gust of wind.

bonds

It takes more effort
To break our morning embrace
Than to raise the dawn.

Ours to Bear

Where are your feet
And how do you know the dropping feeling in the pit of
your stomach isn't proof
That you're falling, fast, arms out in a bear hug?

Reaching 'round the whole planet like a baby's first stretch
outside the womb,
Like the last pterodactyl taking flight
Like every Christ the church still hasn't taken off the cross

My God, my God
Why?

Whatever you do, baby, look down
The bridge is high as fuck, but you don't want to miss this
view

Get on the roller coaster
Even though you're definitely gonna puke your guts out
No one gets off with a full stomach, after all

Superego

The librarian refuses to speak
But needs to be heard.
Tries to stave off her words by
Eating book after book until
They stain her stomach lining
With all the greyscale letters of the alphabet.
One novel gets lodged in her brainstem
Between the cerebellum and
Her ability to keep quiet and
Imposes on her the knowledge that
If she tries to bite her tongue again
She'll bite it clean off.

IV
Repeat.

The Great Commission

Space is heavy, so
When you get up in the morning,
Always remember to stretch your neck muscles,
Square your shoulders,
Take a few steadying breaths, and
Stand up slowly. That's
A whole universe you've got balanced
On the top of your head,
After all.

About the Author

Camilla Marquette is a librarian and poet who technically lives in California, but who's usually lightyears away. *Dry Swallow* is her first book of poetry.

Connect with Camilla

 @earth.to.camilla

 earth-to-camilla.tumblr.com

www.ingramcontent.com/pod-product-compliance
Lightning Source LLC
Chambersburg PA
CBHW021146020426
42331CB00005B/920